ENGINEERING GENERAL KNOWLEDGE

PART 1

Author

Debarati Dutta

This book is dedicated to my mother

late Dola Dutta

This book will give basic concepts of engineering.

Stress

Force per unit area in a solid. The area is perpendicular to the force for tensile stress and parallel to it for shear stress. Unit:

newtons per square meter (Pascal).

$$\text{Stress} = \frac{\text{applied force}}{\text{cross-sectional area}} \qquad \sigma = \frac{F}{A}$$

Strain
The change in shape or size of a stressed body divided by its original shape or size, e.g. 'linear strain', 'shear strain', 'volumetric strain'.

$$\text{Strain} \quad = \quad \frac{\text{change in length}}{\text{original length}} \qquad \varepsilon = \frac{x}{L}$$

Young's modulus of elasticity

A measure of the rigidity of a material. The ratio of stress to strain in the elastic region.

Young's modulus of elasticity $= \dfrac{\text{stress}}{\text{strain}}$ $E = \dfrac{\sigma}{\varepsilon}$

Stiffness

The ability of a metal, etc., to resist elastic deformation. It is proportional to the appropriate modulus of elasticity.

$$\text{Stiffness} = \frac{\text{force}}{\text{extension}} \qquad k = \frac{F}{\delta}$$

Modulus of rigidity

The ratio of shear stress to shear strain within the elastic limit.

$$\text{Modulus of rigidity} = \frac{\text{shear stress}}{\text{shear strain}} \qquad G = \frac{\tau}{\gamma}$$

Thermal strain's Formula

Strain in a body due to a temperature gradient.

Thermal strain $\varepsilon = \alpha T$

= coefficient of linear expansion x temperature rise

Thermal stress in compound bar

Stress in a body due to a temperature gradient.

$$\sigma_1 = \frac{(\alpha_1 - \alpha_2)E_1 E_2 A_2 T}{(A_1 E_1 + A_2 E_2)}$$

Ultimate tensile strength

The maximum tensile stress a material will withstand before failure.

$$\text{Ultimate tensile strength} = \frac{\text{maximum load}}{\text{original cross-sectional area}}$$

Moment

The moment of a force (or other vector quantity) about a point is the product of the force and the perpendicular distance from the line of action of the force to the point.

Moment = force x perpendicular distance $M = Fd$

$$\frac{\text{stress}}{\text{distance from neutral axis}} = \frac{\text{bending moment}}{\text{second moment of area}} = \frac{\text{Young's modulus}}{\text{radius of curvature}}$$

$$\frac{\sigma}{y} = \frac{M}{I} = \frac{E}{R}$$

Torque

The algebraic sum of couples, or moments of

external forces, about the axis of twist. Also called 'torsional moment'

$$\text{Torque} = \text{force} \times \text{perpendicular distance} \quad T = Fd$$

Power

The rate of doing work. Unit: watt (W).

$$\text{Power} = \text{torque} \times \text{angular velocity} \quad P = T\omega = 2\pi n T$$

Horsepower

Horsepower $1 \ hp = 745.7 \ W$

Angular Torque

Torque = moment of inertia × angular acceleration $T = I\alpha$

$$\frac{\text{shear stress}}{\text{radius}} = \frac{\text{torque}}{\text{polar second moment of area}} = \frac{(\text{rigidity})(\text{angle of twist})}{\text{length}}$$

$$\frac{\tau}{r} = \frac{T}{J} = \frac{G\theta}{L}$$

Average velocity

$$\text{Angular velocity} \quad \omega = \frac{\theta}{t} = 2\pi n$$

Acceleration

The rate of change of velocity with respect to time

$$\text{Acceleration} = \frac{\text{change in velocity}}{\text{time taken}} \qquad a = \frac{v - u}{t}$$

Linear velocity

The rate of change of position of a point with respect to time. Unit: meters per second

$$\text{Linear velocity} \quad v = \omega r$$

Angular velocity

$$\text{Angular velocity} \quad \omega = \frac{\theta}{t} = 2\pi n$$

Linear acceleration

Linear acceleration $a = r\alpha$

Relationships between initial velocity u, final velocity v, displacement s,

time t and constant
acceleration a

$$\begin{cases} v_2 = v_1 + at \\ s = ut + \frac{1}{2}at^2 \\ v^2 = u^2 + 2as \end{cases}$$

Relationships between
initial angular velocity ω1,
final angular velocity ω2,
angle θ, time t and angular
acceleration a

$$\begin{cases} \omega_2 = \omega_1 + \alpha t \\ \theta = \omega_1 t + \frac{1}{2}\alpha t^2 \\ \omega_2^2 = \omega_1^2 + 2\alpha\theta \end{cases}$$

Momentum Formula

The product of mass and velocity of a body, i.e. mv.

$$\text{Momentum} = \text{mass} \times \text{velocity}$$

Impulse Formula

Impulse is defined as the change of momentum produced in either body.

Impulse = applied force x time = change in momentum

Force

That quantity which produces acceleration in a body measured by the rate of change of momentum. Unit: newton (N).

Force = mass × acceleration $F = ma$

Weight

Weight = mass × gravitational field $W = mg$

Centripetal acceleration

Centripetal acceleration $\quad a = \dfrac{v^2}{r}$

Centripetal force

A body constrained to move in a curved path reacts with a force (centrifugal force) directed away from the center of curvature. It is equal and opposite to the force deviating the body from a straight line called the 'centripetal force'. Both are equal to the mass multiplied by the 'centripetal acceleration'.

$$\text{Centripetal force} \quad F = \frac{mv^2}{r}$$

Density

The mass of a unit volume of a substance. The unit is kilograms per meter cubed.

$$\text{Density} = \frac{\text{mass}}{\text{volume}} \qquad \rho = \frac{m}{V}$$

Work done

Work done $=$ force x distance moved $W = Fs$

Efficiency

A non-dimensional measure of the perfection of a piece of equipment, e.g. for an engine, the ratio of power produced to the energy rate of the fuel consumed, expressed as a fraction or as a percentage.

$$\text{Efficiency} = \frac{\text{useful output energy}}{\text{input energy}}$$

Power

The rate of doing work. Unit: watt (W).

$$\text{Power} = \frac{\text{energy used (or work done)}}{\text{time taken}} \qquad P = \frac{E}{t} = Fv$$
$$= \text{force} \times \text{velocity}$$

Potential energy & kinetic energy

The capacity of a body for doing work. Types are: kinetic, potential, pressure, chemical, electric, etc.

Potential energy = weight × change in height $E_p = mgh$

kinetic energy = $\frac{1}{2}$ × mass × (speed)^2 $E_k = \frac{1}{2} mv^2$

Kinetic energy of rotation

kinetic energy of rotation
$$= \frac{1}{2} \times \text{moment of inertia} \times (\text{angular velocity})^2 \quad E_k = \frac{1}{2} I \omega^2$$

Frictional force

Frictional force = coefficient of friction × normal force $\quad F = \mu N$

Angle of repose

Angle of repose, θ, on an inclined plane $\tan \theta = \mu$

Efficiency of screw jack

Efficiency of screw jack $\eta = \dfrac{\tan \theta}{\tan(\lambda + \theta)}$

SHM Equations

SHM periodic time $T = 2\pi\sqrt{\dfrac{\text{displacement}}{\text{acceleration}}}$ $\qquad T = 2\pi\sqrt{\dfrac{y}{a}}$

$$T = 2\pi\sqrt{\dfrac{\text{mass}}{\text{stiffness}}} \qquad T = 2\pi\sqrt{\dfrac{m}{k}}$$

Simple pendulum

simple pendulum $\quad T = 2\pi\sqrt{\dfrac{L}{g}}$

Compound pendulum

compound pendulum $T = 2\pi\sqrt{\dfrac{(k_G^2 + h^2)}{gh}}$

Force ratio

$$\text{Force ratio} = \frac{\text{load}}{\text{effort}}$$

Movement ratio

$$\text{Movement ratio} = \frac{\text{distance moved by effort}}{\text{distance moved by load}}$$

Efficiency

$$\text{Efficiency} = \frac{\text{force ratio}}{\text{movement ratio}}$$

Kelvin temperature

Kelvin temperature = degrees Celsius + 273

Quantity of heat energy

Quantity of heat energy $Q = mc(t_2 - t_1)$

$=$ mass $\times$ specific heat capacity $\times$ change in temperature

New length

New length $=$ original length $+$ expansion $\quad L_2 = L_1[1 + \alpha(t_2 - t_1)]$

New surface area equations

New surface area = original surface area + increase in

$$A_2 = A_1[1 + \beta(t_2 - t_1)] \quad \text{area}$$

New volume

New volume = original volume + increase in volume $V_2 = V_1[1 + \gamma(t_2 - t_1)]$

Pressure

At a point in a fluid, pressure is the force per unit area acting in all directions. That is, it is a scalar quantity; e.g. in a cylinder with a piston, pressure P is the force on the piston divided by the cylinder area.

$$\text{Pressure} = \frac{\text{force}}{\text{area}}$$

$$= \text{density} \times \text{gravitational acceleration} \times \text{height}$$

$$p = \frac{F}{A}$$

$$p = \rho g h$$

$$1 \text{ bar} = 10^5 \text{Pa}$$

Absolute pressure

Absolute pressure = gauge pressure + atmospheric pressure

Metacentric height, GM

Metacentric height, GM $GM = \dfrac{Px}{W}\cot\theta$

Bernoulli's equation

Bernoulli's equation $\dfrac{P_1}{\rho} + \dfrac{v_1^2}{2} + gz_1 = \dfrac{P_2}{\rho} + \dfrac{v_2^2}{2} + g(z_2 + h_f)$

Coefficient of discharge

The rate of actual to theoretical flow of a fluid through an orifice, nozzle, Venturi meter, etc.

Coefficient of discharge $C_d = C_v \times C_c$

Characteristic gas equation formula

Characteristic gas equation

$$\frac{p_1 V_1}{T_1} = \frac{p_2 V_2}{T_2} = k$$

$$pV = mRT$$

The indicated power of an IC engine (briefly written as I.P.) is the power actually developed by the engine cylinder. Mathematically,

$$I.P. = \frac{100 \, K \, p_m \, L \, A \, n}{60} \text{ kW}$$

where

K = Number of cylinders,
pm = Actual mean effective pressure in bar (1 bar = 100 kN/m2),
L = Length of stroke in meters,
A = Area of the piston in m2,
n = Number of working strokes per minute
 = Speed of the engine for two stroke cycle engine
 = Half the speed of the

engine for four stroke cycle engine.

Note : The I.P. of a multi-cylinder of spark ignition engine is determined by *Morse test*.

The brake power (briefly written as B.P.) of an IC Engine is the power available at the crankshaft. The brake power of an I.C. engine is, usually, measured by means of a brake mechanism (prony brake or rope brake).

In case of prony brake, brake power of the engine,

$$\text{B.P.} = \frac{\text{Torque in N-m} \times \text{Angle turned in radians through 1 revolution}}{60} \quad \text{(in watts)}$$

$$= \frac{T \times 2\pi N}{60} = \frac{Wl \times 2\pi N}{60} \text{ watts}$$

where

W = Brake load in newtons,
l = Length of arm in metres,
and
N = Speed of the engine in r.p.m.

In case of rope brake, brake power of the engine,

$$B.P. = \frac{(W-S)\pi D N}{60} \text{ watts}$$

$$= \frac{(W-S)\pi (D+d) N}{60} \text{ watts} \qquad ...[\text{Considering diameter } (d) \text{ of the rope}]$$

where
W = Dead load in newtons,
S = Spring balance reading in newtons,
D = Diameter of the brake

drum in metres,
d = Diameter of the rope in
metres, and
N = Speed of the engine in
r.p.m.

Note : The brake power
(B.P.) of an engine is always
less than the indicated
power (I.P.) of an engine,
because some power is lost
in overcoming the engine

friction (known as frictional power). Mathematically,

Frictional power, F.P. = I.P. — B.P.

The total pressure is defined as the force exerted by a static fluid on a surface (either plane or curved) when the fluid comes in contact with the surface. This force is always normal to the surface. The center of pressure is defined as the point of application of the resultant pressure on the surface.

The total pressure and center of pressure on the

immersed surfaces are as follows:

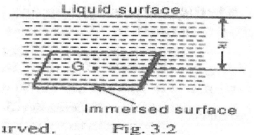

Liquid surface

G

Immersed surface

ırved.   Fig. 3.2

1. Horizontally immersed surface. The total pressure on a horizontally immersed surface, as shown in Fig. 3.2, is given

by

$$P = w A . \bar{x}$$

where

w = Specific weight of the liquid,

A = Area of the immersed

surface, and x (bar) = Depth of the centre of gravity of the immersed surface from the liquid surface.

The above expression holds good for all surfaces whether flat or curved.

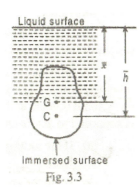

Liquid surface

$\bar{x}$

$\bar{h}$

G

C

Immersed surface

Fig. 3.3

2. Vertically immersed surface.

The total pressure on a vertically immersed surface, as shown in Fig. 3.3 , is given by

$$P = wA.\bar{x}$$

and the depth of centre of pressure from the liquid surface,

$$\bar{h} = \frac{I_G}{A\bar{x}} + \bar{x}.$$

where

A = Area of immersed surface,

$\bar{x}$ = Depth of centre of gravity of the immersed surface from the liquid surface, and

I_g = Moment of inertia of immersed surface about the

horizontal axis through its centre of gravity.

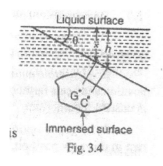

Fig. 3.4

3.   Inclined immersed surface. The total pressure on an inclined surface, as shown in Fig. 3.4, is given by

$$P = w.A.\bar{x}$$

and the depth of centre of pressure from the liquid surface,

$$\bar{h} = \frac{I_G \sin^2 \theta}{A\bar{x}} + \bar{x}$$

where

Theeta = Angle at which the immersed surface is inclined with the liquid surface.

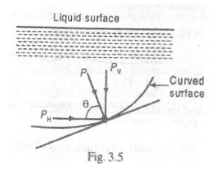

Fig. 3.5

4. Curved immersed surface. The total force on the curved surface, as shown in Fig. 3.5, is given by

$$P = \sqrt{(P_H)^2 + (P_V)^2}$$

and the direction of the resultant force on the curved surface with the horizontal is given   by

$$\tan \theta = \frac{P_v}{P_H} \quad \text{or} \quad \theta = \tan^{-1}\left[\frac{P_v}{P_H}\right]$$

where

PH = Horizontal force on the curved surface and is equal to the total pressure on the projected area of the curved surface on the vertical plane, and

P_v = Vertical force on the curved surface and is equal to the weight of the liquid supported by the curved surface upto the liquid surface.

The bench work and fitting play an important role in every engineering workshop to complete and finish the job to the desired accuracy. The work carried out by hand at the bench is called bench work, whereas fitting is the assembling of parts together by filing, chipping, sawing, scraping, tapping etc., necessary after the machine operation. The various tools used in fitting practice are as follows:

1. Holding tools:

The holding tools or vices are required to hold the work firmly. The various types of vices for different purposes are bench vice, hand vice, pipe vice, leg vice and pin vice.

2. Striking tools:

The striking tools or hammers are used to strike the job or tool. The various types of hammers in common use are ball-peen hammer, cross-peen hammer, straight-peen hammer, double-faced hammer, and soft hammer.

3. Cutting tools:

The chief cutting tools used in fitting are cold chisels, hacksaws and files. These tools are discussed, in brief, as follows:

(a) Cold chisels. These are used to cut the cold metal and are made by forging from cast tool steel of octagonal cross-section. The cutting edge is ground to an angle suited to the material being worked upon. After forging to shape and roughly grinding, the cutting edge should be hardened and tempered. The most commonly used cutting angle is 60°, but this varies according to the type of material cut. The various types of chisels commonly used for fitting are flat chisel, cross-cut chisel or cape chisel, half-round chisel, diamond pointed chisel and side chisel.

(b) Hacksaws. The hacksaw is the chief tool used by the fitter for cutting rods, bars, and pipes into desired lengths. The cutting blades of hacksaw are made of carbon or high-speed steel.

The blades are specified by its length and the point or pitch. The length of the blade is the distance between the outside edges of the holes which fit over the pins. The point or pitch is measured by the number of teeth per 25 mm length. The points of the teeth are bent to cut a wide groove and prevents the body of the blade from rubbing or jamming in the saw cut. This bending of the teeth to the sides is called the setting of the teeth. Usually, alternate teeth are set to right and left, every third or fifth tooth left straight to break up the chips and help the teeth to clear themselves.

(c) Files. A file is a hardened piece of high-grade steel with slanting rows of teeth. It is used to cut, smooth or fit metal parts. The size of the file is indicated by its length. It may be noted that coarseness or pitch of the file varies directly as the length of the file. Thus, larger the length of the file, coarser will be the pitch and smaller the file, finer will be the pitch.

4. Marking, Measuring and Testing tools:

The various marking, measuring and testing tools are Engineer's steel rule, outside and inside calipers, divider, surface plate, scriber, universal surface gauge, punch, V-block, angle plate, try square, combination set etc.

IC Engiine.

The efficiency of an IC engine (Internal Combustion Engine) is defined as the ratio of workdone to the energy supplied to an engine. The following efficiencies of an 1.C. engine are important:

(a) Mechanical efficiency. It is the ratio of brake power (B.P.) to the indicated power (I.P.).

Mathematically, mechanical efficiency,

$$\eta_m = \frac{B.P.}{I.P.}$$

Since B. P. is always less than I.P. , therefore mechanical efficiency is always less than unity (i.e. 100%).

(b) Overall efficiency. It is

the ratio of the work obtained at the crankshaft in a given time to the energy supplied by the fuel during the same time. Mathematically, overall efficiency,

$$\eta_o = \frac{B.P. \times 3600}{m_f \times C}$$

where

B.P. = Brake power in kW, mf = Mass of fuel consumed in kg per hour, and C = Calorific valve of fuel in kJ / kg of fuel.

(c) Indicated thermal efficiency. It is the ratio of the heat equivalent to one kW hour to the heat in the fuel per I.P. hour,

Mathematically, indicated thermal efficiency,

$$\eta_i = \frac{\text{Heat equivalent to one kW hour}}{\text{Heat in fuel per I.P. hour}} = \frac{\text{I.P.} \times 3600}{m_f \times C}$$

Note : The following ratio is Known as specific fuel consumption per I.P. hour:

$$\frac{m_f}{\text{I.P.}}$$

(d)   Brake   thermal efficiency. It is the ratio of the heat equivalent to one kW hour to the heat in the fuel   per   B.P.   hour. Mathematically,   brake thermal   efficiency,

$$\eta_b = \frac{\text{Heat equivalent to one kW hour}}{\text{Heat in fuel per B.P. hour}} = \frac{\text{B.P.} \times 3600}{m_f \times C}$$

Note: The following ratio is known   as   specific   fuel consumption per B. P. hour:

(e) Air standard efficiency. The general expression for the air standard efficiency is given as

(For petrol engines)

$$\eta_{air} = 1 - \frac{1}{r^{\gamma-1}}$$

(For diesel engines)

$$= 1 - \frac{1}{r^{\gamma-1}} \left[\frac{\rho^{\gamma} - 1}{\gamma(\rho - 1)} \right]$$

r = Compression ratio,

γ = Ratio of specific heats, and

ρ = Cut-off ratio.

(f) Relative efficiency. It is also known as efficiency ratio. The relative efficiency of an I. C. engine is the ratio of the indicated thermal efficiency to the air standard efficiency.

(g) Volumetric efficiency. It is the ratio of the actual volume of charge admitted during the suction stroke at N.T.P to the swept volume of the piston.

Slope Calculation:

- Slope (as a percentage) = (Vertical Distance / Horizontal Distance) × 100
- Slope (as a ratio) = Vertical Distance: Horizontal Distance

Earthwork Calculation:

- Volume of Cut or Fill = Average Cross-sectional Area × Length

- Average Cross-sectional Area = (Area 1 + Area 2) / 2

Steel Quantity Calculation:

- Steel Quantity = (Length of Bar × Number of Bars × Weight of Steel per Unit Length) / 1000

- Weight of Steel per Unit Length = (Diameter^2 × π) / 162.198 (for steel bars in kg/m, where diameter is in mm)

Unit Weight:
- Unit Weight of Steel = 7850 kg/m^3

- Unit Weight of Concrete = 2400 kg/m³
- Unit Weight of Brick = 1600-2000 kg/m³ (depending on type)

Load Bearing Capacity:
- Bearing Capacity = (Ultimate Bearing Capacity × Factor of Safety) / Unit Weight of Soil

Slab Load Calculation:
- Slab Load = Dead Load + Live Load

Cantilever Beam Deflection:

- Deflection = (Point Load × Length^3) / (3 × Elastic Modulus × Moment of Inertia)

Moment of Inertia:

- Rectangle: I = (Width × Height^3) / 12
- Circle: I = (π × Diameter^4) / 64

Section Modulus:

- Rectangle: $Z = (\text{Width} \times \text{Height}^2) / 6$

Bending Moment:
- Simply Supported Beam: $M = (\text{Point Load} \times \text{Length}) / 4$

Shear Force:
- Simply Supported Beam: $V = \text{Point Load} / 2$

Bricks Calculation:

- Number of Bricks = (Wall Volume × 1000) / (Brick Volume + Mortar Volume)

Dry Material Quantity for Mortar:

- Cement Quantity = (Mortar Volume × Cement Ratio) / Sum of Ratios

- Sand Quantity = (Mortar Volume × Sand Ratio) / Sum of Ratios

Wet Mortar Volume:
- Wet Mortar Volume = Dry Mortar Volume × 1.3 (approximately)

Excavation Calculation:

- Excavation Volume = Trench Length × Trench Width × Trench Depth

Retaining Wall Stability:
- Factor of Safety against Sliding = (Resisting Force × Wall Length) / (Driving Force × Wall Height)

One-way Slab Thickness:

- Thickness = (Span / Ratio) + (Clear Cover + Main Bar Diameter / 2)

$Weight, W = mg$ $Specific$ $volume, v = V$ $m = 1$ ρ $m3$ kg $Specific$ $gravity, SG = \dfrac{\rho}{\rho H2O}$

Where m=mass, g=gravitational acceleration.

$$Pgage = PAbs - Patm$$
$$Pvac = Patm - Pabs$$
$$Pbelow = Pabove + \rho g \Delta z$$
$$Pgage = \rho gh \quad P = Patm + \rho gh$$

$$KE = mV2\ 2 \quad (kJ) \quad ke = V2\ 2$$
$(kJ\ kg)$ Kinetic Energy: Where m=mass, V=velocity

$$PE = mgz \quad (kJ) \quad pe = gz \quad (kJ\ kg)$$ Potential

Energy: Where m=mass, g=gravitational acceleration, z=elevation ENERGY

TRANSFER BY WORK:

Sign convention: Work done on a system = (+)
Work done by a system = (-)
Electrical

Work: $We=VN$ When N

Coulombs of electrical charge move through a potential difference V In the rate form,

$$\dot{W}_e = VI = I^2 R = \frac{V^2}{R} \qquad (W)$$

Where $\dot{W}_e$ is the electrical power and I is the current.

Electrical work done during a time interval Δt: $W_e = \int_1^2 VI \, dt$ (kJ) Or when V and

I remain constant during interval Δt:

$$We = VI\, \Delta t \qquad (kJ)$$

Mechanical Forms of Work:
$W = Fs \qquad (kJ)$ Work done by a constant force, F on a body displaced a distance s
$W = \int F\, ds$

(kJ) Shaft Work:

$$W_{sh} = 2\pi n T \qquad (kW)$$

Where n is the number of revolutions per unit time

Spring Work:

$$W_{spring} = \frac{1}{2} k \left(x_2^2 - x_1^2 \right)$$

(kJ) Where x1 and x2 are the initial and final displacements of the spring.

Boundary Work: $W_b = \int_1^2 P\,dv$

(kJ) $W_b = P(V_2 - V_1)$

Constant P process:

$$W_b = \frac{P_2 V_2 - P_1 V_1}{1-n}$$

Polytropic process:

$$W_b = \frac{mR(T_2 - T_1)}{1-n}$$

Polytropic Ideal Gas process: $W_b = PV \ln \frac{V_2}{V_1} = mRT_o \ln \frac{V_2}{V_1}$ Polytropic Isothermal Ideal Gas process:

During actual exp/comp process of gases, P and V are related by $PV^n = C$.

Where n and C are constants therefore between 2 states, ideal gas, closed $C = P1V1 = P2V2 = mRT0$ $\therefore \frac{V2}{V1} = \frac{P2}{P1}$ $c_v = \frac{\delta u}{\delta T}\bigg|_v$ SPECIFIC HEAT RELATIONS FOR IDEAL GAS: $c_p = \frac{\delta h}{\delta T}\bigg|_p$ $\Delta u = u2 - u1 = \int_1^2 c_v T dT$ (kJ/kg) $\Delta h = h2 - h1 = \int_1^2 c_p T dT$ (kJ/kg) Variation of spec. heats with T is smooth and may be approx. as linear over small T interval. Can replace specific heat with Cavg, yielding:

$$u2-u1=cv,avgT2-T1 \; ,$$
$$h2-h1=cp,avg(T2-T1)$$
$$cp=cv+R \quad kJ \; kgK \; , \; k-cp \; cv$$

INTERNAL ENERGY, ENTHALPY & SPECIFIC HEATS OF SOLIDS & LIQUIDS

$\Delta u = u2 - u1 = c_{avg}T2 - T1$ $(kJ \; kg)$ $cp = cv = c$ For an incompressible substance: $\Delta h = \Delta u + v\Delta P \cong c_{avg}T2 - T1 + v\Delta P$ $(kJ \; kg)$

IDEAL RANKINE cycle

HEAT ENGINES HEAT PUMP: REFRIGERATOR:

The objective of a HP is to keep a warm space warm

The objective of a Refrigerator is to keep a cold space cold $\eta_{th} = \dfrac{W_{net,out}}{Q_{in}} = 1 - \dfrac{Q_{out}}{Q_{in}}$

$W_{net,out} = Q_{in} - Q_{out}$

Thermal Efficiency of HE, η_{th} Coefficient of Performance for HP, COPHP

$COP_{HP} = \dfrac{Desired\ output}{Required\ input} = \dfrac{Q_H}{W_{net,in}}$

$COP_{HP} = \dfrac{Q_H}{Q_H - Q_L} = \dfrac{1}{1 - Q_L/Q_H}$

$COPHP = COPR + 1$

$COPR = \dfrac{\text{Desired output}}{\text{Required input}} = \dfrac{Q_l}{W_{net,in}}$

$COPR = \dfrac{Q_l}{Q_H - Q_L} = \dfrac{1}{Q_L/Q_H - 1}$ CARNOT HE CYCLE $\eta_{th} = \eta_{th,REV}$ $> \eta_{th,REV}$ $< \eta_{th,REV}$

Irreversible HE Reversible HE Impossible HE CARNOT REFIGERATION CYCLE

$COPR,REV = \dfrac{1}{T_L/T_H - 1}$

CARNOT REFRIGERATOR CARNOT HEAT PUMP:

$$COPHP,REV= \frac{1}{1-TL/TH} \quad \frac{QH}{QL}_{REV} =\frac{TL}{TH}$$

CARNOT HEAT ENGINE:

$$\eta th,REV=1-\frac{TL}{TH}$$

ENERGY BALANCE: CLOSED SYSTEM

$$\Delta Esys=Ein-Eout$$
$$\Delta U+\Delta KE+\Delta PE=Ein-Eout$$
$$m\left[u2-u1 +\frac{1}{2}m\left(V2^2-V1^2\right)\right]$$

$$+mgz2-z1$$
$$=(Qin+Win)-(Qout+Wout)$$

Expanding both the left and right side of the equation:

SIMPLIFY ENERGY

BALANCE FOR CLOSED SYSTEM

Step 1: Define system of interest and simplify E-bal.
Step 2: If Stationary then

$\Box KE = \Box PE = 0$

Step 3: Determine if have Qin or $Qout$ if Adiabatic $\Box Q = 0$ Step 4: Determine if have Wb , Wpaddle, Welectrical ENERGY BALANCE:

OPEN SYSTEM, STEADY STATE $\Delta Esys = Ein - Eout$ $0 = Ein - Eout$ $Qin + Win +$ $m(h + V2\ 2\ in$

$$+gz) = Qout + Wout + m(h + \frac{V2}{2} in + gz)$$

Expanding the equation: MASS BALANCE: OPEN SYSTEM, STEADY STATE $\Delta msys = m\ in - m\ out$ $0 = m\ in - m\ out$ Since $\Box msys = 0$ for SS Since $\Box Esys = 0$ for SS *mass flow rate,* $m = \rho VA$ $V\ in = V\ out$ For Steady, incompressible flow:

Volumetric flow rate, $V = VA = m/\rho$ ENERGY BALANCE: OPEN SYSTEM, UNSTEADY-FLOW

$\Delta E sys = Ein - Eout$

$\Delta U + \Delta KE + \Delta PE = Ein - Eout$

$\Delta U + \Delta KE + \Delta PE = Qin + Win + m(h + V2\ 2\ in + gz) - (Qout + Wout + m(h + V2\ 2\ in + gz))$

Expanding the equation:
MASS BALANCE: OPEN SYSTEM, UNSTEADY-FLOW $\Delta m_{sys} = m\ in - m\ out$
$(m2-m1) = m\ in - m\ out$

INCREASE OF ENTROPY

PRINCIPLE: $\Delta S_{SYS} = S2 - S1 = \delta Q\ T + S_{gen}\ 2\ 1$ ENTROPY, S: $dS = \delta Q\ T\ INT\ REV$ (kJ K)

FIND THE CHANGE IN ENTROPY: $\Delta S = S2 - S1 = \delta Q\ T$

INT REV 2 1   (kJ K)

INTERNALLY REVERSIBLE ISOTHERMAL HEAT TRANSFER : $\Delta S = Q\ T0$
(kJ K) $Sgen$ =0
<0   >0 Irreversible
Reversible

Impossible ISENTROPIC PROCESS: A internally reversible, adiabatic process $\Delta S=0$ or $S2=S1$ (kJ kg K)

ENTROPY CHANGE OF

LIQUIDS AND SOLIDS: $S2-S1=cavg ln T2\ T1 =0$ $T1=T2$ Where cavg is the average specific heat of the substance over the given

temperature interval $S_2 - S_1 =$
$\int_1^2 c(T) \, \dfrac{dT}{T} \cong c_{avg} \ln \dfrac{T_2}{T_1}$
$(kJ \, kg \, K)$

SPECIAL CASE: ISENTROPIC LIQUIDS & SOLIDS ENTROPY CHANGE OF IDEAL GAS: CONSTANT SPECIFIC HEAT

$S_2 - S_1 = c_{v,avg} \ln \dfrac{T_2}{T_1} + R \ln \dfrac{v_2}{v_1}$ $(kJ \, kg \, K)$

$S_2 - S_1 = c_{p,avg} \ln \dfrac{T_2}{T_1}$

$-R \ln P_2 \, P_1$ (kJ kg K)
(Approximate Analysis: for when $\square T$ is small < 300°)

ENTROPY CHANGE OF IDEAL GAS: VARIABLE SPECIFIC HEAT

$S_2 - S_1 = S°_2 - S°_1 - R \ln P_2 \, P_1$ (kJ kg K) (Exact Analysis: for when $\square T$ is large & specific heats vary non-linearly w/in T range)

ISENTROPIC PROCESS OF IDEAL GAS: CONSTANT SPECIFIC HEAT ISENTROPIC PROCESS OF IDEAL GAS: VARIABLE SPECIFIC HEAT

$$\frac{T2}{T1}\bigg|_{S=CONST} = \left(\frac{v2}{v1}\right)^{k-1}$$

$$\frac{T2}{T1}\bigg|_{S=CONST} = \left(\frac{P2}{P1}\right)^{(k-1)/K}$$

$$\frac{P2}{P1}\bigg|_{S=CONST} = \left(\frac{v1}{v2}\right)^{k} \qquad R/cv=k-1$$

$$\frac{P2}{P1}\bigg|_{S=CONST} = \frac{Pr2}{Pr1}$$

$$\frac{v2}{v1}\bigg|_{S=CONST} = \frac{vr2}{vr1}$$

ISENTROPIC EFFICIENCIES OF STEADY-

FLOW DEVICES TURBINE

$\eta_T = \dfrac{\text{Actual Turbine Work}}{\text{Isentropic Turbine Work}} = \dfrac{w_a}{w_s} \cong \dfrac{h_1 - h_{2a}}{h_1 - h_{2s}}$

$\eta_T = \dfrac{\text{Isentropic Compressor Work}}{\text{Actual Compressor Work}} = \dfrac{w_s}{w_a} \cong \dfrac{h_{2s} - h_1}{h_{2a} - h_1}$

COMPRESSOR

$$\square P = w_s \quad w_a = v(P_2 - P_1) \quad h_{2a} - h_1$$

PUMP

$$\square N = \frac{Actual\ KE\ a\ nozzle\ exit}{Isentropic\ KE\ at\ nozzle\ exit} = \frac{V_{2a}^2}{V_{2S}^2} = \frac{h_1 - h_{2a}}{h_1 - h_{2s}}$$

NOZZLE

GENERAL ENTROPY BALANCE

$$\Delta S_{sys} = S_{in} - S_{out} + S_{gen}$$

Mechanisms of Entropy Transfer = Q and m
ENTROPY BALANCE: CLOSED SYSTEM

$$\Delta S sys = S2 - S1 = \frac{Q_K}{T_K} + S gen$$

ENTROPY BALANCE: ADIABATIC CLOSED SYSTEM $\Delta S sys = S gen$
ENTROPY BALANCE: ADIABATIC CLOSED

SYSTEM AND SURROUNDINGS $Sgen=$

$\Delta S=\Delta Ssystem+\Delta Ssurroundings$ $\Delta Ssur=Qsurr$ $Tsurr$

Heat Loss by Thermal Conduction

Formula:

$$\frac{Q}{t} = \frac{kA(T2 - T1)}{d}$$

Q = Amount of heat transferred

t = Time

k = Thermal conductivity of the material

A = Area

T1 = Temperature on one side the material

T2 = Temperature on the other side

d = Thickness of material.

**Heat Loss by Thermal Radiation –
 Stefan-Boltzmann Law**

Formula:

$$P = e\sigma A(T^4 - Tc^4)$$

P = Net radiated power

e = Emissivity (1 for an ideal radiator)

o = Stefan's constant (5.6703×10^{-8} watt/m^{2}K^4)

A = Radiated area

T = Temperature of radiator

Tc = Temperature of surroundings

Thermal Convection – Newton's Law of Cooling

Formula:

$$q = h_c A \, dT$$

q = heat transferred per unit time (W, Btu/hr)

A = heat transfer area of the surface (m^2, ft^2)

h_c = convective heat transfer coefficient of the process ($W/(m^2K)$ or $W/(m^2\,^{\circ}C)$, $Btu/(ft^2\,h\,^{\circ}F)$)

dT = temperature difference between the surface and the bulk fluid (K or $^{\circ}C$, F)

MA = Number of teeth on output gear Number of teeth

on input gear $VR = \dfrac{\text{Number of teeth on input gear}}{\text{Number of teeth on output gear}}$

6.2.3 Belt and pulley systems

$MA = \dfrac{\text{Diameter of output pulley}}{\text{Diameter of input pulley}}$

$VR = \dfrac{\text{Diameter of input pulley}}{\text{Diameter of output pulley}}$

6.3 Dynamics

Newton's equation force = mass x acceleration ($FF = mmaa$)

Gravitational potential energy (Wp) = mass x gravitational acceleration x height (mgh) Kinetic energy (Wk) = ½ mass x velocity2 (1 2 Work done = force x distance (Fs) Instantaneous power = force x velocity (Fv)

Average power = work done / time $(\frac{W}{t})$ m mvv2)

Friction Force ≤ coefficient of friction x normal contact force $(F \leq \mu\mu\mu\mu)$

Momentum of a body = mass x velocity (mv)

Pressure = force / area $(\frac{F}{A})$ 12

Non-flow energy equation $U1 + Q = U2 + W$ so $Q = (U2 - U1) + W$ where Q = energy entering the system W = energy leaving the system U1 = initial energy in the system U2 = final energy in the system. Steady flow energy equation $Q = (W2 - W1) + W$ where Q = heat energy supplied to the system W1 = energy entering the system W2 = energy leaving the system W = work done by the system. 13 14 7.

Thermal Physics p – pressure V – volume C – constant T – absolute temperature n – number of moles of a gas R – the gas constant Boyle's law $ppVV=CC$ $pp1VV1=pp2VV2$

Charles' law $VV\ TT = CC$

$VV1\ TT1 = VV2\ TT2$

Pressure law $pp\ TT = CC$

$pp1\ TT1 = pp2\ TT2$

Combined gas law $pp1VV1\ TT1 = pp2VV2\ TT2$ Ideal gas law $ppVV = nnVVnn$

Characteristic gas law $ppVV = mmVVnn$ where m = mass of specific gas and R = specific gas constant

Efficiency η=work output work input

Heat formulae Latent heat formula Heat absorbed or emitted during a change of state, $Q = mL$ where $Q =$ Energy, L = latent heat of transformation, m = mass

Sensible heat formula Heat energy, $Q = mc\Delta T$ where Q = Energy, m = mass, c =

specific heat capacity of substance, ΔT is change in temperature.

'

Fluid:

Conservation of Mass (Continuity Equation)

$$\frac{\partial}{\partial t} \int_{CV} \rho \, d\Psi + \int_{CS} \rho \vec{V} \cdot d\vec{A} = 0$$

$$\nabla \cdot \rho \vec{V} + \frac{\partial \rho}{\partial t} = 0$$

$$\frac{\partial \rho u}{\partial x} + \frac{\partial \rho v}{\partial y} + \frac{\partial \rho w}{\partial z} + \frac{\partial \rho}{\partial t} = 0$$

$$\frac{1}{r}\frac{\partial(r\rho V_r)}{\partial r} + \frac{1}{r}\frac{\partial(\rho V_\theta)}{\partial \theta} + \frac{\partial(\rho V_z)}{\partial z} + \frac{\partial \rho}{\partial t} = 0$$

Stream Function for Two-Dimensional Incompressible Flow (Cylindrical Coordinates)

$$\frac{\partial(rV_r)}{\partial r} + \frac{\partial V_\theta}{\partial \theta} = 0$$

$$V_r \equiv \frac{1}{r}\frac{\partial \psi}{\partial \theta} \quad \text{and} \quad V_\theta \equiv -\frac{\partial \psi}{\partial r}$$

Momentum Equation for Inertial Control Volume with *Rectilinear Acceleration*

$$\vec{F}_S + \vec{F}_B - \int_{CV} \vec{a}_{rf}\, \rho\, d\Psi = \frac{\partial}{\partial t}\int_{CV} \vec{V}_{xyz}\, \rho\, d\Psi + \int_{CS} \vec{V}_{xyz}\, \rho \vec{V}_{xyz} \cdot d\vec{A}$$

For a *Newtonian* fluid: Shear Stress =

$$\tau_{yx} = \mu\, \frac{du}{dy}$$

Where μ is the dynamic viscosity of the fluid.

$$y' = y_c + \frac{I_{\hat{x}\hat{x}}}{Ay_c}$$

$$x' = x_c + \frac{I_{\hat{x}\hat{y}}}{Ay_c}$$

Thank you.

www.ingramcontent.com/pod-product-compliance
Lightning Source LLC
Chambersburg PA
CBHW031242050326
40690CB00007B/912